S0-AYO-220

PETS' GUIDES

Bunny's Guide to Caring for Your Rabbit

Anita Ganeri

Heinemann
LIBRARY
Chicago, Illinois

To contact Capstone Global Library please phone 800-747-4992, or visit our website www.capstonepub.com

Edited by Daniel Nunn, Rebecca Rissman, and Sian Smith
Designed by Cynthia Della-Rovere
Original illustrations © Capstone Global Library Ltd 2013
Illustrated by Rick Peterson
Picture research by Tracy Cummins
Production by Victoria Fitzgerald
Originated by Capstone Global Library Ltd
Printed in the United States of America in North Mankato, Minnesota. 012014 007944RP

17 16 15 14
10 9 8 7 6 5 4 3

Library of Congress Cataloging-in-Publication Data
Ganeri, Anita, 1961-
Bunny's guide to caring for your rabbit / Anita Ganeri.—1st ed.
        p. cm.—(Pets' guides)
Includes bibliographical references and index.

ISBN 978-1-4329-7135-9 (hb)—ISBN 978-1-4329-7142-7 (pb) 1. Rabbits—Juvenile literature. I. Title.

SF453.2.G36 2013
632'.6932—dc23   2012017417

Acknowledgments
The author and publisher are grateful to the following for permission to reproduce copyright material: Capstone Library pp. 7, 11 (Karon Dubke), 17 left, 19, 21 (Tudor Photography); Corbis pp. 15 (© amanaimages), 27 (© Jutta Klee/ableimages); iStockphoto p. 9 (© christopherarndt); Shutterstock pp. 5 (© Cora Mueller), 25 (© foto Arts); Superstock p. 13 (© imagebroker.net); Ros Lamb pp.17 right, p23 (Kween Betty Winzer).

Cover photograph of a Lop-eared baby rabbit reproduced with permission of Getty Images (Geoff du Feu). Design elements reproduced with permission of Shutterstock (© Picsfive) and Shutterstock (© R-studio).

We would like to thank Ros Lamb, Rae Todd, and the team at the Rabbit Welfare Association & Fund for their invaluable help in the preparation of this book.

Every effort has been made to contact copyright holders of any material reproduced in this book. Any omissions will be rectified in subsequent printings if notice is given to the publisher.

All the Internet addresses (URLs) given in this book were valid at the time of going to press. However, due to the dynamic nature of the Internet, some addresses may have changed, or sites may have changed or ceased to exist since publication. While the author and publisher regret any inconvenience this may cause readers, no responsibility for any such changes can be accepted by either the author or the publisher.

Contents

Some words are shown in bold, **like this**. You can find out what they mean by looking in the glossary.

Do You Want a Pet Rabbit?

Hi! I'm Bunny the rabbit, and this book is all about rabbits just like me! Did you know that rabbits make great pets? We are lively and friendly. But you need to give us lots of care and attention.

Being a good pet owner means making sure that I have food, water, and somewhere clean and safe to live. Then I'll quickly become your best friend.

Choosing Your Rabbit

We rabbits come in all shapes and sizes, from giant to very small. Our coats can be black, white, brown, gray, or a mixture of any of these colors.

Animal shelters often have rabbits that need a good home. You can also buy rabbits from rabbit **breeders** or from good pet shops.

A Healthy Rabbit

Pick a rabbit that looks active and healthy. It should have clean teeth that are not too long, a shiny coat, clean ears, and bright eyes—just like me!

Rabbits get lonely if we live on our own so please get me a friend. It's best to keep a pair of rabbits together. They should both be **neutered**. Otherwise, you may end up with lots of baby rabbits to look after, too.

Getting Ready

Before you bring me home, there are a few things that you need to get ready. This will help make me feel safer and happier when I arrive. Here is my ready-made rabbit shopping list…

Bunny's Shopping List

- a large rabbit house
- shredded paper or hay for bedding
- newspaper and wood shavings for the floor
- a **drip-feeder** water bottle and food bowls
- rabbit food and rabbit toys
- a large **run** that I can play in

My New Home

Rabbits like me need a large house with a living room, a bedroom, and a **run** to play in. Shredded paper or hay makes a cozy bed. I also need a separate place where I can go to the bathroom.

Put my house somewhere dry and away from **drafts**. I can live indoors or outdoors. If I live outdoors, make sure you make my home warm in winter. Otherwise, I'll be f-f-freezing cold.

Home, Sweet Home!

It's time for you to take me home! Use a strong, plastic carrier, with holes in it so that I can breathe. Then put me in my new house and leave me to explore for a while.

I like being stroked, but I don't really like to be picked up. Always ask an adult to pick me up for you. They should put one hand under my chest and the other around my bottom, then lift me up. If I start to struggle, put me down gently.

Dinner Time

I've had a good look around my new house, and now I'm hungry! To stay healthy, I need to eat lots of hay and grass with some juicy dandelion leaves. I need a few good quality **pellets** every day, too.

pellets

Bunny's Top Meal-Time Tips

- Make sure that I always have hay and clean drinking water.

- Check which plants you give me. Some plants make me sick.

- Only give me small pieces of carrot or fruit as a treat.

Time for Play

Like all rabbits, I'm very active and need lots of exercise. Otherwise, I'll soon get bored. A large, fenced-in **run** in the backyard is the ideal place for me to hop around and explore. I should be able to use it whenever I want to.

The run needs a strong wire mesh fence and roof, so that I can't escape and cats and foxes can't get in. Add some logs and tubes for me to explore and a sand pit for me to dig in.

Cleaning My House

Nobody likes a dirty home, so please keep my house clean. Every day, take away wet bedding and droppings, and wash out my food bowls and water bottle.

Clean out my whole house once or twice a week. Then, every few weeks, wash it out with warm, soapy water. Don't forget to wash your hands afterward.

Fur and Teeth

To keep my fur clean, I groom it with my paws, but you can help by brushing me once a week. If your rabbit has long hair, brush it every day to stop its fur from getting tangled.

Why do rabbits have such long front teeth? It's because they grow all the time. If they get too long, I can't eat, so make sure that I have plenty of hay and grass to chew on. This will help to keep my teeth short.

Visiting the Vet

If I stop eating my food, have a runny nose or eyes, or a dirty bottom, I might not be well. Please take me to the vet at once. The vet will examine me and find out what's wrong.

I also need a checkup twice a year. The vet will give me **vaccinations** to stop me from getting bad diseases. You can also get some drops to put on my fur to stop me from getting **fleas** or **mites**.

Vacation Care

You can't take me with you on vacation. If someone else comes to look after me, make sure they have experience in caring for rabbits properly.

If you don't know anyone who can take care of me, you should find me a **boarding home** to stay in while you are away. Make sure they are used to keeping rabbits so that I can enjoy my vacations, too.

Rabbit Facts

- Wild rabbits live in large groups. They dig lots of underground burrows and tunnels, called **warrens**. Fifty or more rabbits can live in a warren.

- Rabbits have long, strong back legs. They stand up to look out for **predators** and thump their feet on the ground to warn others of danger.

- The Flemish giant is the biggest pet rabbit. It can weigh around 18 pounds and is about the size of a small dog.

- Rabbits have to eat some of their own droppings, to help them digest the tough grass and hay that they eat.

Helpful Tips

- Make sure that your rabbit is picked up and handled from an early age. This helps your pet to get used to human contact and not feel scared.

- If you keep two or more rabbits, make sure that each one has a place to go to get away from the others. Otherwise, they may get unhappy and sick.

- Rabbits love digging. Make sure that your pet has somewhere to dig, such as a digging box filled with earth or child-friendly sand.

- A change in your rabbit's usual behavior may mean that he or she is not well. If you are worried, take your rabbit to the vet.

Glossary

boarding home a place where you can leave your pet when you go on vacation

breeders people who have rabbits that need new homes

drafts blasts of cold air that come through a window or under a door

drip-feeder a bottle that is attached to a rabbit's cage and lets water slowly drip out

fleas tiny insects that can live on a rabbit's skin and fur

mites tiny creatures that can live on a rabbit's fur and inside its ears

neutered when a rabbit has an operation, which means it cannot have babies

pellets small lumps of food

predators animals that hunt and eat others for food

run an outside space where a rabbit can run and hop around

vaccinations medicines given by a vet through a needle to stop rabbits from catching diseases

warrens underground burrows and tunnels that wild rabbits live in

Find Out More

Books

Johnson, Samantha. *The Rabbit Book: A Guide to Raising and Showing Rabbits*. Minneapolis: Voyageur Press, 2012.

Maass, Sarah. *Caring for Your Rabbit*. Mankato, Minn.: Capstone Press, 2007.

Internet Sites

Facthound offers a safe, fun way to find Internet sites related to this book. All of the sites on Facthound have been researched by our staff.

Here's all you do: Visit www.facthound.com Type in this code: 9781432971359

Index